FOCUS ON

WATER

BARBARA TAYLOR

SHOOTING STAR PRESS

This edition produced in **1995** for
Shooting Star Press Inc
Suite 1212, 230 Fifth Avenue
New York, NY 10001

© Aladdin Books Ltd 1994

Created and produced by
Aladdin Books Ltd
28 Percy Street
London W1P 9FF

*First published in
the United States in 1995 by*
Shooting Star Press Inc

ISBN 1-57335-153-9

Design	David West Children's Book Design
Designer	Flick Killerby
Series director	Bibby Whittaker
Editor	Richard Green
Picture research	Brooks Krikler Research
Illustrator	Dave Burroughs

The author, Barbara Taylor, has a degree in science, and has written and edited many books for children, mainly on science subjects.

The consultant, Dr. Bryson Gore, is a lecturer and lecturers' superintendent at The Royal Institution, London.

INTRODUCTION

Without water, life as we know it would be impossible and our world would not exist. Water has many unique properties – it keeps us alive, helps us transport goods and people from place to place, it stops the Earth from getting too hot or too cold and its power can be harnessed to produce electricity. Water has a major influence on the weather and climate of the earth, as well as continually changing the shape of the land. The amount of water on earth has stayed the same for thousands of millions of years and will not change in the future. This book explores the scientific properties of water and aims to provide a complete picture of where water comes from, how we use it, and its importance to life on earth.

Geography
The symbol of the planet earth shows where geographical facts are examined in this book. These sections discuss how water affects people's lives around the world, and how it shapes the land in different ways.

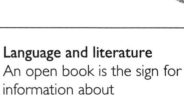

Language and literature
An open book is the sign for information about language and literature. Legends about mermaids and the mystery of the lost continent of Atlantis are among the subjects discussed in these sections.

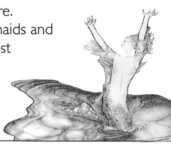

Science, math and technology

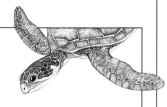

The microscope symbol indicates where scientific information and activities are included. Hydro-electric power and artificial rain making are examined in these boxes. A green-tinted symbol signals an environmental issue.

History

The sign of the scroll and hourglass shows where historical information is given. How the Romans used water and a look at the history of water transport are included in these sections.

Social history

The symbol of the family signals information about social history. These sections explain how the weather and living near water affects people's homes around the world, and the significance of water in religious ceremonies.

Arts, crafts and music

A symbol showing a sheet of music and art tools signals where information and activities about arts, crafts and music is given. The importance of water as a source of inspiration to famous artists is discussed in one of these sections.

CONTENTS

WHAT IS WATER?

Water is not only one of the most common substances on earth, it is also one of the most unusual. Unlike any other substance, water exists as a solid, liquid and gas in everyday life. Each drop of water is made up of millions of molecules (tiny particles). Water molecules consist of even smaller particles called atoms. Two atoms of hydrogen combine with one atom of oxygen to form the chemical compound H_2O (water). Over 70 per cent of the earth's surface is covered by water. Water is everywhere – it fills oceans, rivers, lakes, soaks into the ground and is even present in the air that we breathe.

Forms of water

Water can exist in three different forms – as a solid, a liquid and a gas. The form water takes depends on how fast the molecules of H_2O move. In ice (right), the molecules are tightly bound and move slowly. However, in its liquid form, water molecules can move more quickly. The molecules in water vapor (a gas) move faster still and travel freely in the air.

When you breathe out on a cold day, the water vapor in your breath cools down and turns into droplets of liquid water, which form a mist in the air.

Salt water

About 97 per cent of the world's water is the salty water in the seas and oceans. Seawater is "salty" because it contains minerals and salts washed off the land and carried to the sea by rivers. Objects float more easily in salt water than in fresh water. The salt makes the water "thicker" or more dense. The Dead Sea (below), in the Middle East, is about eight times more salty than seawater, allowing bathers to float with ease.

Beliefs and ceremonies

Water is a powerful symbol of purity and cleanliness, and is used in many religious ceremonies around the world. Hindus believe the sacred River Ganges, in northern India, cleanses their souls as well as their bodies, and transports the dead to heaven. The bathing ghats at Varanasi, on the banks of the Ganges, have been used by Hindu pilgrims (right) for thousands of years. In the Christian ceremony of baptism, holy water is sprinkled on to a person's head, to mark the start of their new life as a Christian.

Life in water

The first life on earth probably evolved from simple chemicals on the surface of early oceans about 3,500 million years ago. Today, the oceans contain about 20 per cent of all the animal species on Earth and watery environments on land, such as marshes and swamps – wetlands – are especially rich in wildlife. One of the largest wetlands in Europe are the salty marshes and shallow lakes of the Carmargue Nature Reserve in southern France. The grazing of the famous white horses helps to maintain the marshes by stopping trees and scrub taking over. Tens of thousands of wildfowl migrate here for the winter months. Colonies of pink flamingos (shown left) breed in the summer months, despite the industry, housing and airports which surround the park borders.

Water words

There are many sayings which include the word water. To "be in deep water," implies being in great difficulties; to "spend money like water," is to spend money recklessly as if you had an endless supply. Do you know the meanings of these sayings: "water under the bridge;" "to be like a fish out of water?"

Water energy

Over the centuries, people have harnessed the energy of moving water using water-wheels, and more recently, with hydro-electric power plants or wave and tidal power stations. Water power is a form of renewable energy – it does not use up limited resources, such as coal, gas or oil. Water is often seen as a clean energy resource as it does not pollute the air or produce dangerous toxic waste. However, water power can cause serious environmental problems. Dams alter the landscape and tidal barrages destroy estuaries which are often very rich in wildlife.

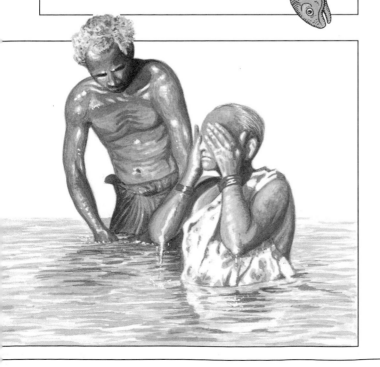

WATER IN HISTORY

When people first began to live in towns and cities, they built their homes near water. They needed water for agriculture and transport as well as drinking, washing, cooking and dumping rubbish. From coastal cities, ancient peoples set sail to explore new lands and trade their goods. The first great civilizations all developed in the valleys of major rivers, such as the Nile in Egypt, the Tigris-Euphrates in modern day Iraq, and the Huang He in China.

The legend of Atlantis
A famous Greek legend tells of a great island civilisation of Atlantis which mysteriously disappeared into the sea. Some historians think the legend relates to the volcanic eruption on the island of Santorini, in the Mediterranean, in 1470 BC. The eruption was so violent that it caused a huge tidal wave and earthquakes. These probably destroyed the rich Minoan civilization on the island of Crete. Other people have suggested that the Azores and the Canary Islands are all that is left of the lost civilisation of Atlantis. The Atlantic Ocean is probably named after Atlantis.

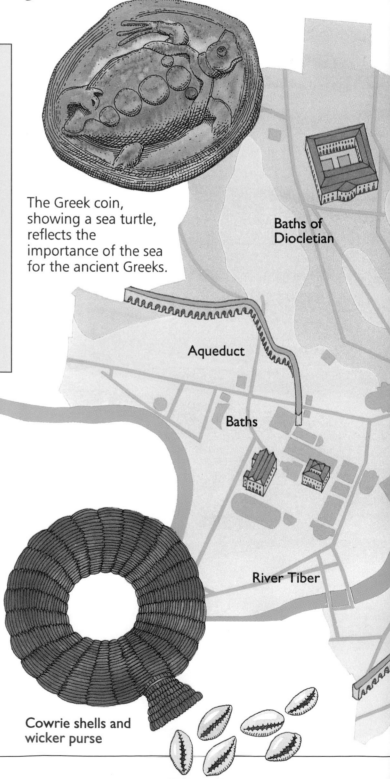

The Greek coin, showing a sea turtle, reflects the importance of the sea for the ancient Greeks.

Baths of Diocletian

Aqueduct

Baths

River Tiber

Ancient Rome
The ancient city of Rome, in Italy, grew up at the easiest crossing point of the River Tiber. Two thousand years ago, the ancient Romans recognized the importance of water and built houses with running water, sewers, aqueducts, public baths, canals and reservoirs throughout their empire. Historians have calculated that the Romans used about five times as much water as the people of London, England, do today.

Some ancient societies exchanged shells or stones for the goods they needed. Cowrie shells, like these (right), are sometimes still used as money today in the Pacific Islands. The wicker purse is for carrying the shells.

Cowrie shells and wicker purse

The wealth of the Nile

Over 5,000 years ago, the ancient Egyptian civilization grew up on the banks of the River Nile. The soil near the river was very good for growing crops because each year, the river burst its banks depositing fertile, black soil for about six miles on either side of the river (shown right).

The Egyptians based their entire agricultural system around this annual flooding.

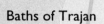

Baths of Trajan

Aqueduct

Baths of Caracalla

Baths of Decius

The Sumerian civilization grew up between the Euphrates and Tigris rivers (shown left in modern day Iraq), about 6,000 years ago. The two rivers flooded in early summer and the Sumerians built a system of canals to drain the land and irrigate their fields.

By AD 284, there were around 1,000 private bathhouses and 11 public baths in Imperial Rome. The largest and most impressive were opened by the emperors Caracalla and Diocletian.

Make a water clock

Thousands of years ago, the Egyptians and the Romans used water to measure time. Water clocks were used in Rome as early as 159 BC. They used containers from which water escaped at a steady rate. As the water fell, it uncovered a scale on the side of the container. See if you can design and make your own water clock like the one shown here. To obtain a steady flow of water, the container needs to have slightly sloping sides. Time how long the water takes to reach each of the levels on your scale. How long does your water clock take to empty?

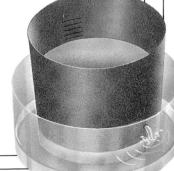

HOW WE USE WATER

In many countries around the world, water is easily available and people tend to take it for granted. Water is used for washing, drinking, cooking, cleaning and central heating systems, as well as for water sports, such as swimming, sailing or waterskiing. In developed countries, such as Europe and North America, people use more than two bathtubs full of water a day. However, in developing countries, where there is little rain and water is not piped to people's homes, water is a precious commodity that has to be saved and used very carefully.

Water and our bodies

Without water people could not survive for more than a few days. Every day, we need about a gallon (3 – 4 liters) of water. We lose a lot of water when we breathe out, sweat and go to the toilet. For instance, during strenuous exercise, runners may lose more than a quart of water through sweating and breathing heavily. When we need more water, our bodies tell us to drink by making us feel thirsty.

Water for life

Poets and painters have often been inspired by water's life-giving properties. Water seems to have a new, fresh, almost magical quality that makes it a powerful symbol of life. The painting *Birth of Venus* (right), by the Italian artist Botticelli, is based on the ancient Greek myth of how Venus, the goddess of beauty, was born in the sea and blown to the shore on a shell.

Water and health

Harmful bacteria live in dirty water and in the waste matter from our bodies which we flush down the toilet. In the Europe of the 1840s, pioneers of public health began to introduce clean water supplies and good sewage systems. Today, because of poor water supplies, many countries still suffer from water-borne diseases, like cholera and typhoid.

Water chart

Do you know how much water you use a day? See if you can work out how much water you use and draw up a chart to record the results. You could measure out drinks in a kitchen measuring jug. Here are some average measurements to help you.

Cleaning your teeth – 5 quarts.
Flushing the toilet - 2.3 gallons
Having a shower - 3.5 gallons per minute
Having a bath - 35 gallons
Washing your face - 5 quarts
Having a drink - 0.7 gallons
Automatic washing machine - 71 gallons

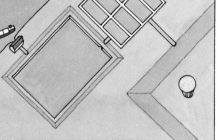

Many people enjoy the recreational uses of water. Popular water sports include swimming, water-skiing, surfing and sailing.

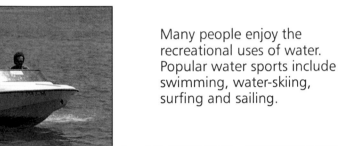

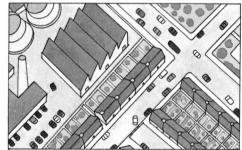

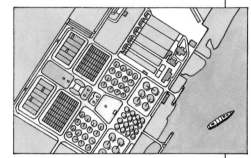

Clean water, dirty water

In many parts of the world, water is cleaned both before and after we use it. Water is taken from rivers (1), wells and reservoirs to a purification plant (2) where it is treated with chemicals, such as chlorine, to kill germs such as bacteria. Water is often stored in water towers (3) before it is pumped to houses and factories (4). After the water has been used, it goes to sewers which deliver it to a sewage treatment works (5). There, harmful dirt and germs are removed before the water is pumped back into the river (6).

Water in developing countries

In developed countries, people use far more water than is necessary to simply stay alive. However, for millions of people in Asia, Africa and South America, clean water is not so easily available. In more than half the households in the world, people have to walk up to four or five miles to the nearest water source to fetch all the water they use. People often carry the water in pots or buckets (shown right) which can sometimes weigh as much as 44 pounds.

WATER AT WORK

From industry to agriculture to generating power for factories and homes, we make water work for us. To make the paper for this book, about 4 gallons of water were used, and other industrial processes, such as making cars, use vast amounts of water. Some power stations use water to generate electricity, while others need large quantities of water to cool machinery – you can often see water vapor escaping into the atmosphere through huge cooling towers (shown above).

Water power

Water generates power when it flows from a higher to a lower place. Water-wheels were originally used to capture the energy of flowing water and use it to turn millstones that ground corn or wheat into flour. Today, turbines use moving water to generate electricity. Modern turbines are huge machines weighing thousands of tons. They are usually placed at the bottom of a dam to make the best use of the energy made by falling water.

Water-wheel

The Itaipú Dam (shown above), on the Paraná River in Brazil, is one of the world's largest hydro-electric dams. Its 18 turbines can produce 13 million kilowatts of electricity.

Industry

In the USA, industry uses around 320 million gallons of water each day. Water is used for washing, cleaning, cooling, dissolving substances and even for transporting materials, such as logs for the timber industry (above). About 7,100 gallons of water are needed to make a car and eight quarts of water are used to produce just one quart of lemonade. The largest industrial users of water are paper, petroleum, chemicals and the iron and steel-making industries.

Dam problems

Dams can cause problems for people and for the environment. Before a dam is built, people and animals have to be cleared from the area. If trees or plants are left to rot under the water, they make the water acidic and the acid may corrode (eat away) the machinery inside the dam. Reservoirs may become clogged by mud and silt which cannot be washed away downstream.

Flood irrigation is used to grow rice. The fields of young rice plants are flooded, covering them in water. These fields are called paddy fields (above). It takes about 9,900 pounds of water to grow just one pound of rice.

An Archimedes screw lifts water up a spiral screw to a higher level. The device was invented by the Greek scientist Archimedes over 2,000 years ago. It is still used in some parts of the world today.

Irrigation
Crop plants, such as wheat or rice, need large quantities of water to grow properly. In places where there is not enough water, or the supply varies with the seasons, farmers irrigate the land. Most irrigation systems involve a network of canals and ditches to carry water to the crops. The sprinkler irrigation system (below) has an engine and wheels and moves across a field spraying crops with a fine mist of water.

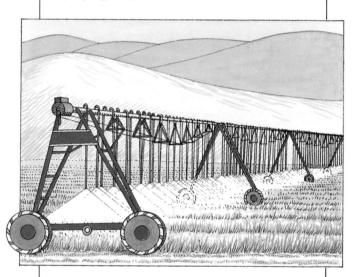

Hydroponics
Plants can be grown without soil using a watering technique called hydroponics. A carefully controlled mixture of nutrients are dissolved in water and passed over the roots of plants which are suspended in a tank of water. Hydroponics does not produce better or larger crops, but it is important in the study of plants and can be used in areas where soil is not easily available, such as on board a ship or in Arctic areas.

Solar salt
For centuries, salt has been a vital part in people's diets and has even been used instead of money. In countries such as China, India and France, salt is harvested from seawater and used for food flavoring or to make industrial chemicals. Seawater is left in shallow pools in the hot sun so the water evaporates, or disappears, into the air. Salt crystals are left behind and can be raked by hand or collected by machines. The salt is then taken to a refinery where it is crushed, ground and sorted before being packaged and sold. Evaporating seawater is the oldest method of obtaining salt. This kind of salt is called solar salt.

SHIPS AND BOATS

For over 6,000 years, people have used logs, rafts, boats and ships to transport people and goods around the world. As people began to leave their homes to explore new lands, better ways of building boats and ships developed. Further improvements came with the establishment of trade routes to distant parts of the world. Boats and ships were originally propelled by oars or sails, but steam power took over in the mid-19th century. Today, diesel engines or steam turbines are widely used to power ships, but new forms of propulsion, such as electromagnetism, are also being developed.

Why ships float
When a ship sits in the water, it pushes some water out of the way. This is called displacement. Ships displace a weight of water equal to their own weight. The displaced water pushes back against the sides of the ship with a force called upthrust. This holds the ship up and keeps it afloat. Ships float if the upthrust of the water is strong enough to support their weight. A boat with a hull can carry more weight than a raft. This is because the boat sits lower in the water, creating greater upthrust.

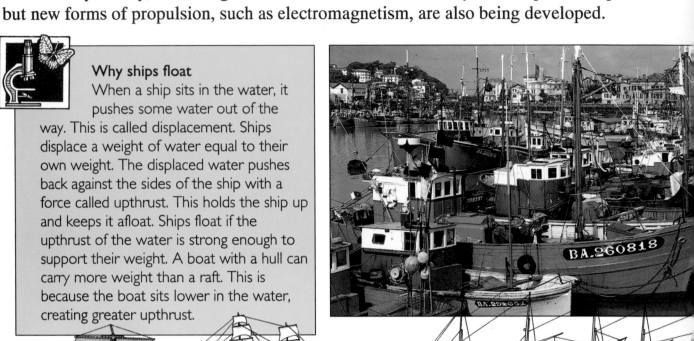

Canoe   Raft   Clipper   Steamship

Trade routes
By the mid-19th century, the development of fast, ocean-going clippers opened up new markets around the world. Luxury goods, such as tea, silks and ivory could be transported from the Far East to Europe in a matter of weeks. In 1869, the Suez Canal (right) was opened, allowing ships to sail across northeast Africa to the Mediterranean. Because there was not enough wind for clippers, steamships took over the trade routes to the Far East.

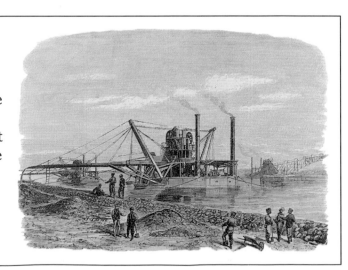

Plimsoll line

The Plimsoll line on the side of a ship shows the safe level for a fully loaded ship in different types of water. A ship floats at different levels depending on the weight of the cargo, the temperature of the water and salinity (how much salt there is in the water).

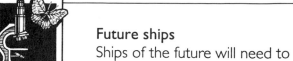

Future ships

Ships of the future will need to have very efficient engines so they can travel further with less fuel. The high cost of fuel, together with environmental considerations, has led to experiments with computerised sail power. Computer controlled sails allow a ship to reduce engine power when there is a favourable wind. Other innovations include a superconducting electro-magnetic ship, called *Yamoto 1* (below), which is being developed by a team of Japanese scientists. It is powered by electromagnets instead of the traditional diesel engine and screw propeller.

Development of shipping

The first boats were probably floating logs or rafts. The ancient Egyptians began using rafts with sails on the Nile as early as 5,000 BC. Boats made of planks of wood allowed the construction of much bigger ocean-going vessels, culminating in the sleek clippers of the mid-1800s. Iron ships, driven by steam engines, replaced sailing ships around 1900. Modern ships are powered by turbines or diesel engines. Hydrofoils lift a ship's hull out of the water, allowing much greater speeds.

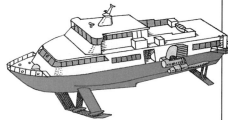

Container ship

Hydrofoil

Canals and locks

Thousands of miles of canals were built at the height of the Industrial Revolution, between 1760 and 1840. Goods, such as coal, were carried by long, narrow boats called barges, pulled by horses walking on a towpath beside the canals. The water in a canal is always level, so to change height, canals have a series of locks (right). Canal transport is still widely used in countries like France and Germany.

LIVING ON WATER

People and animals often build their homes in coastal waters or on rivers and lakes. Living near water is useful for transport, trade and food supplies. Some people even live on houseboats or sampans floating permanently on the water. In the future, as space begins to run out on land, more cities may be built floating on water, or on artificial islands reclaimed from the sea.

In some parts of the world, houses are built on a platform fixed to poles above shallow water. These houses are called pile dwellings; they provide protection against flooding.

Venice

Venice, in Italy, was built on over 100 islands in a lagoon near the Adriatic sea. The foundations of the buildings were built on pine wood piles, driven into the bedrock, and its "streets" are canals (shown right) which crisscross the city. In the 14th century, the city became a wealthy world center for shipping and trade. Today, Venice is a major tourist attraction, but its waters are badly polluted and it is slowly sinking into the Adriatic.

Animal builders

Safety from enemies and a good food supply are reasons why animals build homes on or in water. Beavers build lodges in the middle of rivers. Reed warblers tie their woven nests to reed stems, while caddis fly larvae carry their home of sticks and stones under water. China mark caterpillars live in air spaces inside floating leaves until they turn into adults.

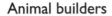

China mark caterpillar

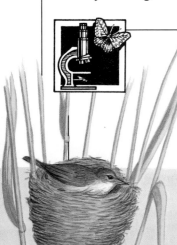

Reed warbler

Caddis fly larvae

Land from the sea

More than one third of the Netherlands is below sea-level. To reclaim land from the sea, engineers built dikes (barriers of earth) around areas of shallow water. Pumps were used to drain out the water, leaving behind fertile areas of land, called polders, which are used for farming. Prins Alexander Polder, the lowest point in the Netherlands, is about 19 feet below sea-level.

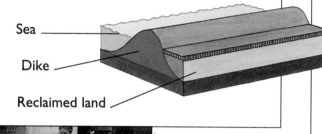

Sea

Dike

Reclaimed land

Bridges

The first bridges were probably made by laying tree trunks across rivers or placing flat stones in shallow streams. Later, people made bridges from rope or built stone bridges with arches. The first bridge known to historians was built in the ancient city of Babylon (in modern day Iraq) about four thousand years ago. Modern bridges are made from concrete, steel or other modern materials. Suspension bridges have thick steel cables that carry the weight of the bridge. They can span long distances because they are lightweight. The Akashi-Kaikyo bridge, in Japan, will be the world's longest suspension bridge whan it is completed in 1998. It will span 11,680 feet.

A new airport is being built on Chep Lap Kok island (left) in Hong Kong. The island will be levelled and then enlarged with about 71 cubic meters of rock and sand.

The Marsh Arabs

People have lived on the marshy land between the Tigris and Euphrates rivers in modern day Iraq for five or six thousand years. The Marsh Arabs of today make reed houses on small, natural islands in the marshes, or make their own artificial islands from mud and reeds.

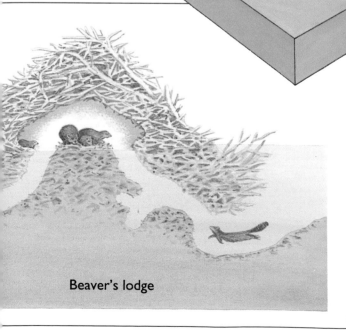

Beaver's lodge

ANIMALS IN WATER

From seas and oceans, to rivers, lakes and ponds, the waters of the earth teem with all sorts of animal life. Fish live in water all the time, while animals, such as frogs, are amphibious (specially adapted to living on land and in water), and only spend part of their life-cycle in water. Some of the largest animals in the world, such as the whale, can only live in water, because it supports their massive body. Ocean currents carry sea mammals, fish and microscopic animals, called zooplankton, around the world. Most animals are adapted to either fresh or salt water, but a few, such as eels and salmon, can survive in both.

Water birds
Ducks, geese and swans have webbed feet which help them swim. Rails and coots have long toes to walk over soft mud without sinking in. Long legs allow herons and storks to wade in deep water.

Animals in shells
Shellfish, such as crabs, limpets and mussels, have strong, hard shells to protect their soft bodies. Crabs are scavengers, eating almost anything edible from the seabed or seashore.

Crab

Mussels

Limpets

Insects
Water bugs, such as water boatmen and water beetles, inhabit freshwater ponds, slow-moving streams and still pools.

Eel

Fish
Roach and bream are freshwater fish which live in lakes and rivers all over Europe. Eels can survive in both salt and fresh water.

Bream

Water boatman

Roach

Sea mammals
Dolphins, sea cows and whales, like this humpback whale (left), spend their whole lives in the water. Thick layers of fat, called blubber, help to keep them warm. They come to the surface to breathe air through a blowhole on the top of the head. Other sea mammals include seals, sea lions and walruses.

Dolphins and porpoises have a smooth, sleek, streamlined shape. Water flows past them easily, allowing them to swim faster.

Mermaids

Mermaids have appeared in stories about the sea for hundreds of years. The top half of a mermaid is like a woman, and the bottom half is like a fish. People used to believe that mermaids lured sailors to their deaths with their beauty and enchanted singing.

Breathing in water

All animals need to take in oxygen, which allows them to release energy from their food. There is oxygen dissolved in water which fish absorb by gulping in water and forcing it over tiny, featherlike structures called gills (shown right). Gills are rich in blood vessels, and oxygen is absorbed directly into the blood and carried around the body. Like other animals which breathe oxygen, fish produce carbon dioxide as a waste product. It passes from the blood through the gills and into the water. Gills or gillike structures, are also found in molluscs (animals in shells), crabs and water insects, such as mayfly nymphs.

Gill

Otter

Mammals

Otters are specially adapted to living both in and out of water. They have soft underfur which traps air, keeping water out and body heat in, and webbed feet for swimming.

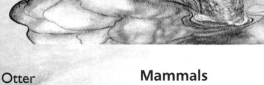

Leeches and medicine

Doctors once believed that too much blood in the body was the cause of some diseases. They put water animals, called leeches, on a patient's body to suck out some of the blood. When a leech feeds, it produces a chemical that stops blood from clotting (thickening). A single leech can rapidly take in three or four times its own weight in blood.

Reptiles

Most reptiles live on land but some, such as sea-turtles, crocodiles and alligators, spend much of their lives in the water, coming to land mainly to lay eggs. Turtles swim with their paddlelike flippers, while crocodiles and alligators use their powerful, flattened tails for swimming.

Crocodiles and turtles are ancient reptiles which have lived in the world's seas and rivers for thousands of years.

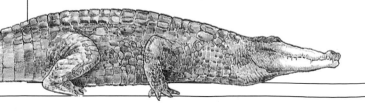

PLANTS AND WATER

Like animals, plants are full of water. Water helps to support land plants so they stay upright and keep their shape. Water is essential for all the chemical processes that keep a plant alive, especially photosynthesis – the process by which plants make food. Water also acts as a transport system, carrying important minerals and nutrients from one part of a plant to another. Plants that live in dry places have special adaptations to store water and prevent water loss. Water plants have the opposite problem – they need to stop themselves becoming waterlogged.

Rising water
You can see how plants take up water by doing this experiment with carnations. Take a white carnation with a short stem and stand it in a container of colored water. Use food coloring to color the water. After several hours, you should be able to see how the flower has taken up the water. The petals will have tints from the food coloring.

Transpiration & photosynthesis
Land plants take in water through their roots and release it into the air through their leaves. Water is drawn upward, through the roots and stem, to the leaves. This is called the transpiration stream, and the evaporation of water from the leaves is called transpiration. Water escapes from the leaves through tiny holes called stomata.

Transpiration helps the plant to cool down, as well as draw up more water from the soil. Unlike animals, plants make their own food by a process called photosynthesis. They contain a green substance, called chlorophyll, which enables plants to use the energy from sunlight to turn carbon dioxide gas from the atmosphere, and minerals and water from the soil, into sugars – the plant's food.

Waxy surfaces
A waxy surface to some leaves seals in water or stops plants absorbing too much water and becoming waterlogged.

Hairy leaves
Hairs on leaves help to trap valuable moisture and stop it escaping into the air.

Spines and needles
Long thin leaves and needles have a smaller surface area and lose less water to the atmosphere than a wide, flat leaf.

Roots
Roots draw up moisture and certain minerals from the soil. Water is absorbed by tiny hairs which cover the roots.

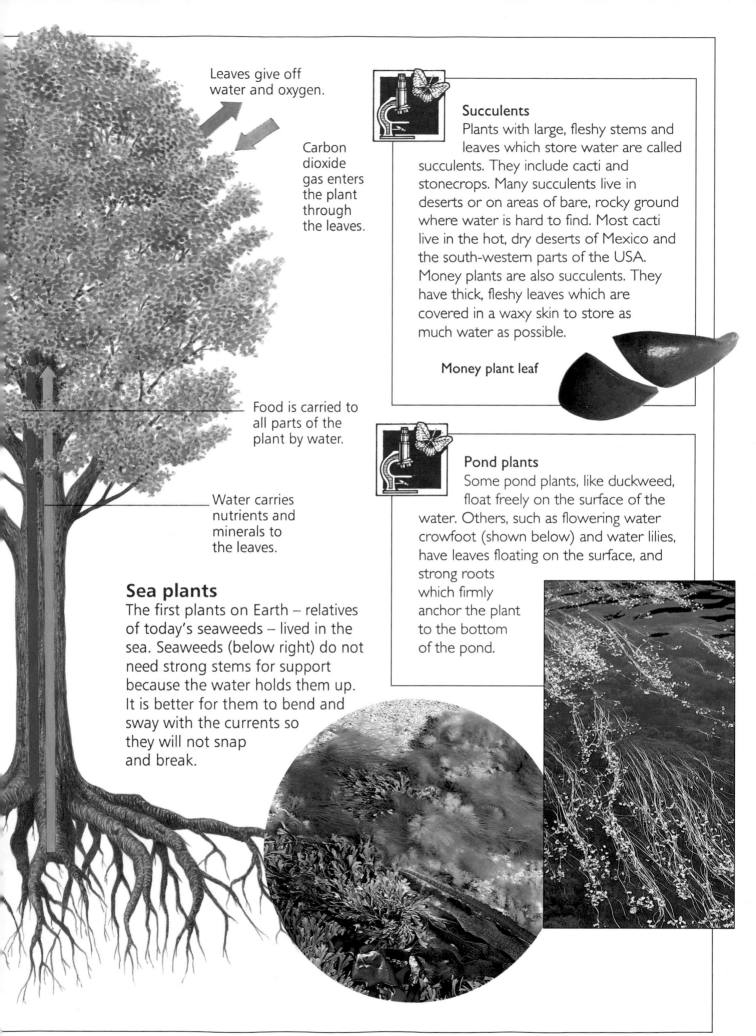

Leaves give off water and oxygen.

Carbon dioxide gas enters the plant through the leaves.

Food is carried to all parts of the plant by water.

Water carries nutrients and minerals to the leaves.

Succulents

Plants with large, fleshy stems and leaves which store water are called succulents. They include cacti and stonecrops. Many succulents live in deserts or on areas of bare, rocky ground where water is hard to find. Most cacti live in the hot, dry deserts of Mexico and the south-western parts of the USA. Money plants are also succulents. They have thick, fleshy leaves which are covered in a waxy skin to store as much water as possible.

Money plant leaf

Pond plants

Some pond plants, like duckweed, float freely on the surface of the water. Others, such as flowering water crowfoot (shown below) and water lilies, have leaves floating on the surface, and strong roots which firmly anchor the plant to the bottom of the pond.

Sea plants

The first plants on Earth – relatives of today's seaweeds – lived in the sea. Seaweeds (below right) do not need strong stems for support because the water holds them up. It is better for them to bend and sway with the currents so they will not snap and break.

SHAPING THE LAND

Water is a powerful force which is constantly changing the shape of the land both above and below ground. It wears away, or erodes, stones, rocks and mountains. Rivers carve valleys, canyons and caves but also build estuaries, deltas and beaches where they meet the sea. Frozen rivers of ice, called glaciers, grind and tear away at rocks, shaping valleys and mountains. Where the sea meets the land, the effect of waves, tides and currents constantly alters the shape of the coastline.

Glacial landscapes

During the history of the Earth, there have been a series of ice ages at regular intervals. Ice sheets spread out from the Poles to cover much more of the Earth than they do today. Clues to the presence of the ice remain long after the ice has melted away. Valleys become U-shaped instead of V-shaped and rocks have scratched or polished surfaces where ice has moved over them. The Briksdal glacier (shown right), in Norway, is one of Europe's largest glaciers.

Rivers

Near the source of a river, the water flows quickly. As the river gathers more water, it flows more slowly, bending from side to side and depositing mud and sand along the riverbanks. Eventually, rivers flow into the sea, dropping the rest of their load of sand and mud to form an estuary or delta.

Delta

Headland

Arch

Sea stack

Coves

Waves at work

Waves wear away land by the sea, using rocks and pebbles as cutting tools. Chemicals in seawater make it slightly acidic, so it eats into rocks, especially soft rocks, such as chalk or limestone. Soft rocks are worn away to form bays, while hard rocks jut out as headlands. Coves on opposite sides of a headland may meet in the middle to form an arch. If the roof of an arch falls in, a column of rock, called a stack, is left standing at the foot of the cliff.

Canyons

In dry areas, where rivers carry water from mountains or rains outside the region, they carve out deep valleys called canyons. One of the most spectacular canyons is the Grand Canyon in Arizona. It is 212.4 miles long and about one mile deep.

Underground caves

Pillar

Stalactite

Stalagmite

The frozen continent

Antarctica contains 90 per cent of the world's ice and most of the Earth's freshwater is locked up in this ice. In the center of the continent, temperatures range from -122°F to -140°F and winds can gust at up to 100 miles per hour (160 kph). In the summer, as the ice around the coast melts, penguins, like these Chinstrap penguins, come ashore to breed on the exposed shoreline.

Underground water

Underground water is slightly acidic and eats into soft rocks, such as limestone, forming tunnels and caves. Eventually, the water may collect into large underground rivers, which erode the rocks still further. As water drips through the cave roof, it evaporates, leaving behind columns of minerals which were dissolved in the rocks. These are called stalagmites (which grow up from the floor) and stalactites (which hang down from the roof). Over hundreds of years, stalagmites and stalactites may meet, forming pillars.

Rivers of the underworld

The ancient Greeks believed there was a kingdom of the dead, called Hades, beneath the Earth. It had five rivers, which were boundaries between the land of the living and the land of the dead. The Styx was the best known river in Hades. To cross the Styx, a soul had to be ferried by a boatman called Charon, who demanded payment for his work. This is why the ancient Greeks placed coins in the mouths of their dead before burying them.

Waterfalls

Waterfalls, like this one in South Wales, often form where rivers flow over layers of hard and soft rock. The soft rock is worn away, leaving behind a step of hard rock, which becomes a steep cliff over thousands of years. The water tumbles over the cliff as a waterfall. Waterfalls may also occur where river valleys have been widened by glaciers.

THE WEATHER

The blanket of air around the earth – the atmosphere – is full of water. Most of the moisture is in the form of an invisible gas, called water vapor. When the air is cool enough, some of the water vapor turns into the tiny water droplets that form clouds, rain, mist and fog. If the temperature near the ground is below freezing, frost and snow may occur. The amount of rain and snow that falls to the ground varies at different times of the year, as the movement of the earth around the sun causes seasonal changes in the weather.

The water cycle

The amount of water on the earth never changes because the water moves round and round in a continuous cycle, called the water cycle. Water is recycled and used over and over again. The warmth of the sun makes the liquid water in rivers, lakes and especially oceans evaporate and rise up into the atmosphere as water vapor. During evaporation from seawater, salt is left behind and the water that rises is freshwater. When this cools down, it changes back into droplets of liquid water, forming clouds. These droplets of water eventually fall back to the earth as rain, sleet or snow. The cycle is completed as the water collects on the ground and in lakes, rivers and oceans.

Monsoon myths

In southeast Asia, there are monsoon rains at certain times of year. These winds are full of moisture from the ocean and bring torrential rainfall. The rains are vital for agriculture. The dragon became a symbol of the monsoon rains to the Chinese. Like the dragon, the rains could be violent and powerful, but were also very important since they brought the precious gift of water.

Weather forecasting

Weather forecasting is a complex process involving satellites, radar and weather stations all over the world. Weather satellites carry television cameras that photograph weather systems around the world. The photograph shown here was taken by a NASA weather satellite and shows the center, or eye, of a tropical storm.

Clouds

Millions of droplets of water or ice floating in the sky make up the clouds we see. There are three main types of cloud – cumulus (meaning heaped), cirrus (feathery), and stratus (layered). Fluffy cumulus clouds are usually a sign of fair weather, while flat blankets of stratus cloud bring rain or drizzle. Large, dark cumulonimbus clouds bring storms while altocumulus (like cotton wool balls) are a clue to unsettled weather to come.

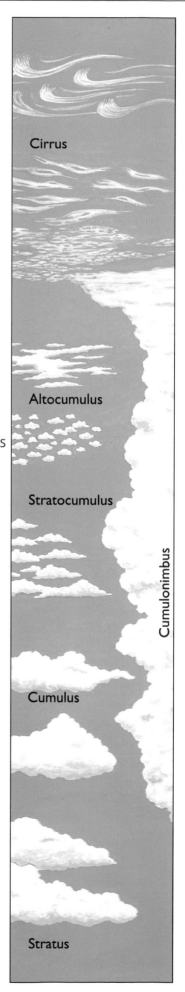

Cirrus

Altocumulus

Stratocumulus

Cumulonimbus

Cumulus

Stratus

Weather damage

The weather can cause a lot of damage to people's homes. Rain and damp air make wood rot unless it is specially protected. If bricks and stones soak up water they crack and crumble. A thick layer of felt or plastic can be placed between bricks a little way above the ground. This damp-proof layer stops water from getting to the bricks above it. In very cold weather, the water in pipes sometimes freezes into ice. As water freezes, it expands and presses against the pipes, causing cracks. When the ice melts, the water pours out of the cracks, and damages the building.

Icicles form when snow or ice melts and freezes again.

FLOODS & DROUGHTS

Too much or too little water can cause terrible damage and loss of life. Floods and droughts can destroy homes, destroy farmland and kill people and wildlife. Hurricanes and earthquakes can cause huge tidal waves, called tsunamis, which can devastate islands and coastal regions. If people store water in artificial lakes or storage tanks they are better able to survive droughts. Dams and flood barriers can give some protection against floods and waves, but so many people live along the coast or near rivers that disasters are bound to occur.

Floods

Floods are caused by too much rainfall in too short a time. Other factors, such as the shape of the land, the amount of water in the ground and whether the ground is frozen also affect the extent of the flood. Great floods are a natural feature of the Lower Mississippi River in North America. Over the past 400 years, floods have happened about once every five years. Despite attempts to control the river, floods still occur.

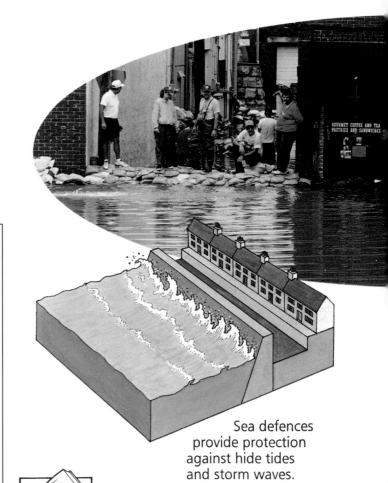

Sea defences provide protection against hide tides and storm waves.

The Thames flood barrier
Dangerous flood conditions are created in the estuary of the River Thames, near London, England, if freak storms suddenly raise the level of the sea. Seawater is channelled into this relatively shallow area, causing a storm surge. The Thames barrier consists of four huge gates which can be closed to seal off the river and prevent floods upstream of the barrier. A storm tide warning service warns the barrier control center of approaching storm surges. Scientists watch for low pressure in the atmosphere, which can cause the sea level to rise.

Noah's ark
The story of Noah's ark has been told all over the world for many generations. When a great flood covered the earth, God is supposed to have told one man, Noah, how to make a wooden ark to save his family and two of every living creature. After 40 days the flood waters retreated and Noah and all the animals came out to begin a new life.

Landslides,

Landslides, such as this one in Scarborough, England, occur on steep slopes when heavy rain or earthquakes cause large amounts of soil to slide down the slope. Landslides are common in parts of Southeast Asia, where earthquakes and volcanic eruptions combine with heavy rainfall to push soil and rock down slopes.

Droughts

A drought is a long period with less than normal rainfall – often this is defined as less than 0.001 inch (0.2mm) of rain over about two weeks. During a drought, rivers and lakes dry up and plants wither and die as soil becomes parched and cracked (shown left).

Desperate measures, such as sand bags and dams, failed to stop the record flooding of the Mississipi River in 1993.

Stormy seas

Storm waves, whipped up by the wind are a spectacular and often terrifying sight, especially for sailors. Many artists, such as the famous English painter J. M. W. Turner, have tried to capture the strength and atmosphere of stormy seas. In the painting Rough Sea (below) Turner tries to portray the power of storm waves and the atmospheric effects of the sky, water and light of a storm at sea. Other paintings, like Winslow Homer's *Gulf Stream*, show the violence and danger of the sea.

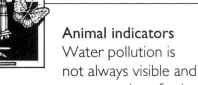

WATER POLLUTION

Water can be polluted by industrial wastes from factories, agricultural chemicals, sewage and household wastes. When people use water for leisure activities, the wake (small waves) from boats can break down river banks and engines leave an oily film on the water's surface. Polluted water can also spread diseases, such as typhoid, cholera and dysentery. Controlling water pollution is expensive but essential if we are to have a clean supply of water in the future.

Animal indicators

Water pollution is not always visible and some species of animal living in water can give clues to the amount of pollution. Bloodworms (above) can stand a lot of pollution while freshwater shrimps and stone-fly nymphs (below) live only in clean water. Rattailed maggots (the larvae of hoverflies) breathe through a snorkellike tube which they stick out of the water into the air. They can live in very polluted water where other animals cannot get enough oxygen to survive.

If sea birds get oil on their feathers, they lose their insulating properties. The animals get very cold and wet and will die if the oil cannot be washed off.

Acid rain

Acid rain is damaging the soil, poisoning lakes and rivers and devastating forests all over Europe and North America. Acid rain is caused by industrial emissions from power stations and vehicle exhaust fumes. Gases, like carbon dioxide, mix with water in the atmosphere to form weak acids. This falls to the ground as acid rain, hail, snow, mist or fog. Acid rain harms or kills trees and plants, poisons rivers, lakes and streams, killing fish and other water creatures. It also affects buildings, causing bricks and stonework to crumble (right).

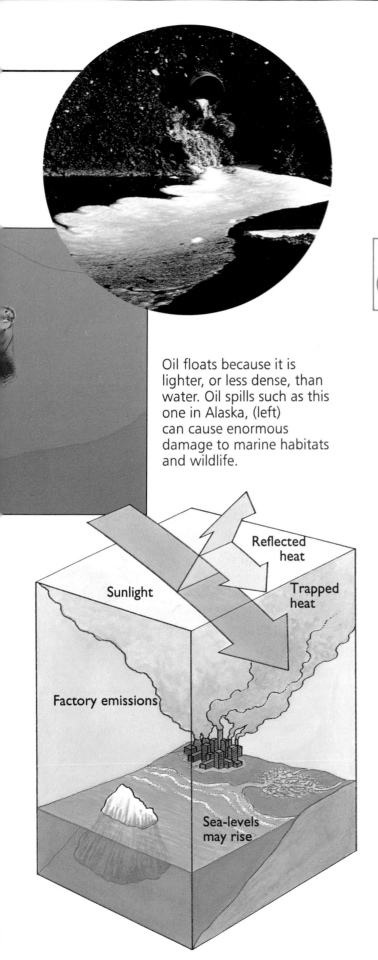

Sewage and toxic waste

Although laws have been passed in many countries to limit the discharge of toxic waste, hazardous chemicals regularly get into lakes and rivers (left). In many countries, huge amounts of sewage are dumped into fresh water and the sea. Like toxic waste, untreated sewage can cause plant and animal life to die and it can also carry dangerous diseases.

Eutrophication

Some chemicals cause pollution, called eutrophication, because they provide living things with too much nourishment. This upsets the balance of life in the water, causing water plants, such as algae, to grow in huge numbers. They block out the light and use up all the oxygen in the water, suffocating and poisoning the fish. The water becomes like a thick green soup with scum on the surface. Chemical fertilizers washed off fields and the phosphates in washing powders can cause this sort of pollution.

Oil floats because it is lighter, or less dense, than water. Oil spills such as this one in Alaska, (left) can cause enormous damage to marine habitats and wildlife.

Reflected heat

Sunlight

Trapped heat

Factory emissions

Sea-levels may rise

Global warming

Many scientists believe that the earth is gradually warming up. This is known as global warming. The earth is kept warm by heat from the sun which is trapped in the atmosphere by certain gases, such as carbon dioxide. Without this, the average temperature would be 86°F (30°C) lower than it is now. However, in recent years, pollution from factories and vehicle exhausts has caused an increase in the amount of heat-trapping gases in the atmosphere. As a result, more heat is trapped which could lead to a rise in world temperatures. This warming could have a dramatic effect on the world's climate. Certain areas could be affected by drought and shortfalls in food production, causing famine. In other places, sealevels may rise, flooding coastal areas. Even more serious is the possibility of the polar ice caps melting if temperatures rise dramatically.

WATER IN THE FUTURE

Water is an abundant energy source and it will be available long after the fossil fuels (coal, gas and oil) have been used up. Water power does not cause environmental problems such as acid rain or global warming. Already, about one-fifth of the world's electricity comes from hydro-electric power and there are plans to use wave and tidal power to produce more energy. Obtaining fresh water from the sea could also become more feasible with new technology. However, all of these projects depend on the careful conservation of water and control of water pollution.

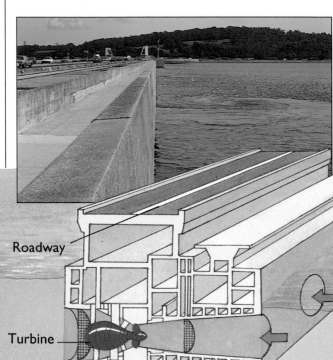

Tidal power

In places where there is a big difference between high and low tide, tidal power could be a major source of energy. In 1966, the world's first tidal power station (left) was built across the mouth of the River Rance in Brittany, France. It generates power when the tide comes in and goes out, providing enough power for a city of about 300,000 people. Tidal power does not cause conventional pollution but it can damage or destroy the rich estuary habitats of many fish and birds.

Roadway

Turbine

The force of the water turns turbines, which are used to generate electricity.

Water enters as the tide rises and leaves as the tide falls.

Water conservation

More and more water is needed as industry and population grows. Water is a vital resource that needs to be managed more carefully. We need to reduce the amount of pollution from industry, agriculture and our homes if we are to ensure a clean, fresh water supply.

Rain making

Sometimes, rain can be "made" by adding substances such as dry ice (frozen carbon dioxide), silver iodide crystals or ammonium nitrate and urea to clouds. These chemicals provide "seeds" around which raindrops or ice crystals can grow. The process works best in clouds from which rain is almost ready to falll. Rain making or cloud seeding can also be used to make rain fall away from large areas of crops and reduce the damage and strength of a storm.

Vehicle fuel
Scientists at the Mazda Motor Corporation in Japan are currently developing a car which uses hydrogen as a source of fuel. The hydrogen is taken from water, which is made up of molecules of hydrogen and oxygen (see page 4). Water is an ideal fuel, as most of the exhaust gases are steam, not polluting gases such as carbon dioxide and sulphur dioxide, which damage the environment.

Mazda's prototype hydrogen car

From salt to fresh water
In places where there is little rain, such as the Middle East, fresh water can be obtained by removing salt from seawater. This is called desalination. A common desalination process is to heat seawater at low pressure. Some of the water forms steam, which condenses into salt free water. Desalination is expensive and no help to cities far from the coast.

Water evaporates

Fresh water collects

Seawater pumped in

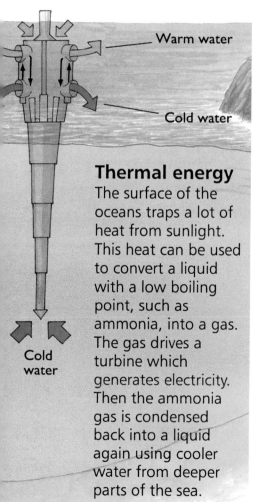

Warm water

Cold water

Thermal energy
The surface of the oceans traps a lot of heat from sunlight. This heat can be used to convert a liquid with a low boiling point, such as ammonia, into a gas. The gas drives a turbine which generates electricity. Then the ammonia gas is condensed back into a liquid again using cooler water from deeper parts of the sea.

Cold water

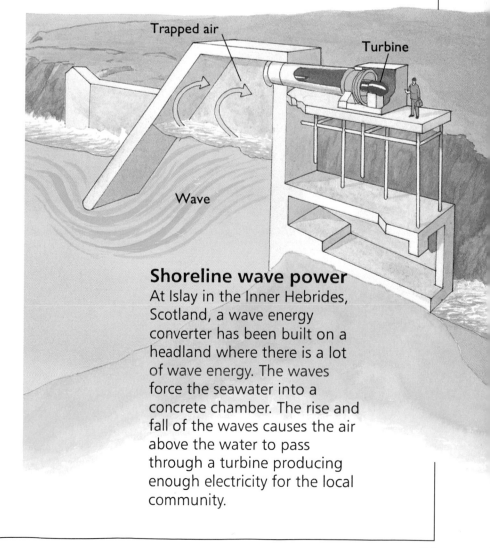

Trapped air

Turbine

Wave

Shoreline wave power
At Islay in the Inner Hebrides, Scotland, a wave energy converter has been built on a headland where there is a lot of wave energy. The waves force the seawater into a concrete chamber. The rise and fall of the waves causes the air above the water to pass through a turbine producing enough electricity for the local community.

WONDERFUL WATER FACTS

On average, a person drinks 14,000 gallons of water during their lifetime.

The Pacific Ocean is bigger than all the earth's land put together. Over half the world's water is in the Pacific Ocean and the other oceans and seas contain most of the rest.

The water we drink is the same water the dinosaurs drank. This is because the water on earth is never used up, it just keeps going round and round, being used over and over again.

If you live in London, England water is drunk by about six other people before you get a drink.

Industrial processes use huge amounts of water: 21,000 gallons are needed to make one ton of paper 83 gallons are needed to make 0.25 gallon of beer; and about 135 gallons of water are used to make the paper for one Sunday newpaper in Britain.

Cucumbers and melons are nearly all water fish fingers and ice cream are more than half water; a tomato is 95 per cent water; sunflower seeds are only 5 per cent water. Human beings are about 65 per cent water and an elephant is about 70 per cent water.

The Huang He, or Yellow River (in northern China), has been nicknamed "China's sorrow" as it has flooded 1,500 times in the last 3,500 years, claiming more lives than any other feature on the earth's surface.

There is enough salt contained in the sea to cover the land with a layer 520 feet thick.

The average person in North America uses about a thousand times as much water as a person in Asia.

The world's smallest flowering plant is a sort of duckweed that floats on water. Twenty-five of these plants would fit across a fingernail.

During the last ice age, the sea-level was about 400 feet lower than it is today. Since then, sea-level has risen by about three inches every 100 years.

One of the largest icebergs ever recorded was estimated to contain enough fresh water to give everyone 20 glasses of water.

The biggest beaver dam on record was 700 feet across on the Jefferson River in North America. Beaver dams are usually only 70-100 feet across.

To produce a quart of milk, a dairy cow must drink about four quarts of water.

GLOSSARY

Acid rain Rain with chemicals from vehicle exhausts or power stations dissolved in it, making it more acidic than normal.

Aqueduct An artificial channel, often on stone pillars above the ground, to carry water.

Climate The average weather in a place over a long period of time.

Clippers Fast, cargo carrying ships of the 18th and 19th centuries.

Condensation The process by which a gas (such as water vapour) turns into a liquid (such as liquid water) as it cools down.

Density The mass (weight) of a substance per unit of volume.

Desalination The process of removing salt from seawater to obtain fresh water fit for people to drink.

Displacement The amount of water or liquid pushed out of the way by a floating object. An object will float if it weighs the same as the liquid it displaces.

Evaporation The process by which a liquid is heated to become a vapor or a gas.

Global warming An increase in the earth's temperature which may be caused by carbon dioxide and other gases stopping heat escaping from the earth. It could lead to rises in sealevels.

Hydro-electric power Electricity that is generated from falling water.

Irrigation To supply crops with extra water when there is not enough rainfall.

Monsoon A wind which blows from different directions at different times of year, causing a wet season and a dry season.

Photosynthesis The process by which plants make food using sunlight, carbon dioxide, water and minerals.

Plimsoll line Marks on the side of a ship showing the safe levels for a fully loaded ship to float in different types of water.

Polder An area of low-lying land reclaimed from the sea, especially in the Netherlands.

Renewable energy Energy sources that are natural and will not run out, such as waves and falling water.

Streamlined Something with a smooth, sleek shape that cuts through air or water easily.

Sumer An area of modern day Iraq, near the Tigris and Euphrates rivers, where people first lived in cities about 3500 BC.

Tides The rise and fall of seawater, twice each day, caused by the pull of the moon's gravity as it circles the earth.

Transpiration The evaporation of water through microscopic holes, called stomata, in plant leaves or stems.

Turbine A machine containing a rotor which is turned by high energy water or steam, used to generate electricity.

Water cycle The neverending way in which water moves around the world, from the oceans to the clouds and back to the oceans again.

Water vapor The invisible gas that water turns into when it is heated.

INDEX

Photographic Credits:

Abbreviations: t-top, m-middle, b-bottom, l-left, r-right
Cover tl, 4b, 5b, 7b, 8m, 10t, 12t & m,16, 20b, 23b, 25t: Spectrum Colour Library; Cover tr, 28b: Charles de Vere; cover b, title p, 2t & m, 4t, 8t, 14t, 18 all,19t & br, 20t & b, 21b, 22 all, 22-23, 23m, 26b: Roger Vlitos; 2b, 3t,12b,17, 25bl: Mary Evans Picture Library; 3b, 8br, 25br: Bridgeman Art Library; 5t, 7t, 10m, 11t, 23t, 24-25, 26t & m, 27: Frank Spooner Pictures; 7m: copyright British Museum; 8bl: Hulton Deutsch; 10b Hutchison Library; 11b, 13b, 14-15, 21t: Eye Ubiquitous; 19bl: Planet Earth Pictures; 28t: Salter; 28m: Science Photo Library; 29: Mazda Cars.